The Complete Clean Eating Cookbook

Healthy whole food recipes and meal plans to kickstart your healthy lifestyle in this beginner's weight loss cookbook

The information in the following pages is broadly considered a truthful and accurate account of facts and as such, any inattention, use, or misuse of the information in question by the reader will render any resulting actions solely under their purview. There are no scenarios in which the publisher or the original author of this work can be in any fashion deemed liable for any hardship or damages that may befall them after undertaking information described herein.

Additionally, the information in the following pages is intended only for informational purposes and should thus be thought of as universal. As befitting its nature, it is presented without assurance regarding its prolonged validity or interim quality. Trademarks that are mentioned are done without written consent and can in no way be considered an endorsement from the trademark holder.

Introduction

Healthy eating is essential for everyone. At clean eating meal prep we understand that everyone has different needs, goals, and preferences. That is why we provide healthy eating meal prep options for individuals to choose from.

Our meal prep options come in the form of ready-to-eat and store-ready meals. They include a wide variety of lean proteins and vegetables. The store-ready items can be picked up at your local grocery store, while the ready-to-eat items are made fresh and frozen daily in our facility.

We put a lot of thought into how to make our meal prep items healthy and appealing while still being easy to prepare. That is why we use no additives or preservatives in our meal prep products. We are committed to providing you with clean, delicious meals every time you order from us.

We all know that a healthy diet is key to maintaining a healthy lifestyle. clean eating meal prep knows that a healthy diet can also be great when you're on the go. That's why we created meal prep kits to help you stay on track with your clean eating goals.

With the clean eating meal prep meal prep kit, you can prepare and store everything you need for your clean eating regimen in one convenient location. You'll be ahead of the game because you'll be prepared for that busy day when you're running around after school, work, or your kids.

Preparing your meals ahead of time will eliminate the temptation to order take out and save yourself from being hungry and unfocused during the day. Plus, it will save you money as well!

"But I don't eat healthy! I need something convenient!" You're not alone.

We get it. Everyone wants to eat healthy without sacrificing the ability to make delicious, nutritious meals.

At clean eating meal prep, we understand. That's why we've created a new meal prep service that makes eating healthy easy to do.

What is Meal Prep? How Does It Work?

Meal prepping is the process of creating an entire day's worth of healthy and nutritious meals ahead of time. This way you can focus on shopping for ingredients, rather than what you plan to cook. Yes, you can still order delivery or eat out, but it is so much easier to make the whole meal at once!

Meal prepping allows you to eat healthy with a lot more flexibility! So say goodbye to go-to foods that are high in refined carbs or just generally unhealthy and hello to fresh, new options!

Being on a clean eating diet is not hard or complicated. It just requires that you eat a lot of real foods and cut out the processed foods and sugar-packed beverages. But if there's one thing most people struggle with when it comes to dieting and meal-prepping, it's knowing what foods to eat and which foods are safe to eat on a clean eating diet. That's where we come in.

With our meal prep service, you don't have to worry about what you're eating. With our convenience delivered daily, you can easily eat real foods with straightforward meal plans listed at easy-to-read calorie amounts. We help you stay on track with our in-depth tracking system so that you know exactly how much protein, fat, carbs and fiber you're getting at every meal.

With clean eating meal prep meal prep, you can be as healthy as possible without having to think too hard about what to eat or when to eat. All you have to do is stop by our retail store or ship us your order for free and get ready for a healthy lifestyle!

30 Day Meal Plan

Day	Breakfast	Mains	Dessert	Snack
1	Leek & Spinach Frittata	Cucumber Avocado Salad with Bacon	Mint Chocolate Chip Ice-cream	Spiced Nuts
2	Cherry Chia Oats	Baked Cod with Cucumber-Dill Salsa	Flourless Sweet Potato Brownies	Easy Guacamole
3	Banana Pancakes	Indian Chicken Curry	Paleo Raspberry Cream Pie	Spicy Bean Dip
4	Baked French Toast Casserole	Persian Chicken	Caramelized Pears	Cashew "Humus"
5	Whole Grain Blueberry Scones	Pesto Pork Chops	Berry Ice Pops	Roasted Garlic Chickpeas
6	Spinach Mushroom Omelet	Roasted Red Pepper and Eggplant Soup	Fruit Cobbler	Salt & Vinegar Kale Crisps
7	Weekend Breakfast Salad	Cilantro-Lime Flounder	Watermelon and Avocado Cream	Sweet Potato Muffins
8	Kale Turmeric Scramble	Seafood Casserole	Coconut and Chocolate Cream	Anti-Inflammatory Key Lime Pie
9	Poached Salmon Egg Toast	Herb Pesto Tuna	Chocolate Bananas	Apple Crisp

10	Egg Muffins with Feta and Quinoa	Grilled Calamari with Lemon and Herbs	Watermelon Sorbet	Apple Sauce Treat
11	Peaches with Honey Almond Ricotta	Traditional Chicken-Vegetable Soup	Cinnamon Apple Chips	Brownies Avocado
12	Quinoa Breakfast Bowl	Arroz Con Pollo	Avocado Brownies	Brussels Sprout Chips
13	Cream Cheese Salmon Toast	Cheesy Chicken and Mushroom Casserole	Fruit Salad	Cauliflower Snacks
14	Chapter 3:	Tuna Casserole	Chocolate Chip Cookies	Cucumber Yogurt
15	Carrot Cake Overnight Oats	Pork Burrito Bowls	Hot Chocolate	Hummus Deviled Eggs
16	Mediterranean Frittata	Slow Cooker Pork Chili	Tropical Popsicles	Hummus with Celery
17	Maple Oatmeal	Pork Stir-Fry	Strawberry Ice Cream	Kale Chips
18	Tomato Omelet	Meaty Lasagna	Blueberry Tarts	Lemony Ginger Cookies
19	Tuna & Sweet Potato Croquettes	Jarlsberg Lunch Omelet	Cookie Dough Bites	Mandarin Cottage Cheese
20	Quinoa & Veggie Croquettes	Mu Shu Lunch Pork	Banana Cinnamon	Mushroom Chips
21	Turkey Burgers	Bacon & Chicken Patties	Banana Cinnamon Cookies	Toasted Pumpkin Seeds
22	Salmon Burgers	Prosciutto Spinach Salad	Avocado Chia Parfait	Tofu Pudding

23	Quinoa & Beans Burgers	Caramelized Pork Chops	Choco Chia Cherry Cream	Turmeric Gummies
24	Veggie Balls	Chicken Bacon Quesadilla	Avocado Choco Cake	Paleo Ginger Spiced Mixed Nuts
25	Coconut & Banana Cookies	Sesame-Crusted Tuna with Green Beans	Date Dough & Walnut Wafer	Easy Peasy Ginger Date
26	Fennel Seeds Cookies	Rosemary Roasted Pork with Cauliflower	Pineapple Pie	Baked Veggie Turmeric Nuggets
27	Almond Scones	Grilled Salmon and Zucchini with Mango Sauce	Citrus Cauliflower Cake	Turmeric Coconut Flour Muffins
28	Oven-Poached Eggs	Beef and Broccoli Stir-Fry	Creamy & Chilly Blueberry Bites	Ginger Flour Banana Ginger Bars
29	Cranberry and Raisins Granola	Parmesan-Crusted Halibut with Asparagus	Pistachioed Panna-Cotta Cocoa	Tangy Turmeric Flavored Florets
30	Spicy Marble Eggs	Hearty Beef and Bacon Casserole	Pure Avocado Pudding	Buttered Banana Chickpea Cookies

Breakfast

Leek & Spinach Frittata

Preparation Time: 10 minutes
Cooking Time: 15 minutes
Servings: 4
Ingredients:

Chapter 1:   2 Leeks, Chopped Fine
Chapter 2:   2 Tablespoons Avocado Oil
Chapter 3:   8 Eggs
Chapter 4:   ½ Teaspoon Garlic Powder
Chapter 5:   ½ Teaspoon Bail, Dried
Chapter 6:   1 Cup Baby Spinach, Fresh & Packed
Chapter 7:   1 Cup Cremini Mushrooms, Sliced
Chapter 8:   Sea Salt & Black Pepper to Taste

Directions:

1. Set the oven to 400°F then get an ovenproof skillet. Place it over medium-high heat, sautéing your leeks in your avocado oil until soft. It should take roughly five minutes
2. Get out a bowl, and whisk the eggs with your garlic, basil, and salt. Add them to the skillet with your leeks, cooking for five minutes. You'll need to stir frequently.
3. Stir in your mushrooms and spinach, seasoning with pepper.
4. Place the skillet in the oven then bake for 10 minutes. Serve warm.

Nutrition:

Calories: 276
Protein: 19 Grams
Fat: 17 Grams
Carbs: 15 Grams

Cherry Chia Oats

Preparation Time: 10 minutes
Cooking Time: 20 minutes
Servings: 2
Ingredients:
1. ¼ Teaspoon Vanilla Extract, Pure
2. 2 Tablespoons Almond Butter
3. 8 Cherries, Fresh, Pitted & Halved
4. 1 Cup Quick Cook Oats
5. 2 Tablespoons Chia Seeds
6. ¼ Cup Whole Milk Yogurt, Plain
7. 1 ¼ Cup Almond Milk

Directions:
1. Mix all of together the ingredients until they're combined well.
2. Seal in two jars and refrigerate for twenty-five minutes before serving.

Nutrition:
Calories: 564
Protein: 22 Grams
Fat: 32 Grams
Carbs: 27 Grams

Banana Pancakes

Preparation Time: 5 minutes
Cooking Time: 15 minutes
Servings: 2
Ingredients:

- 2 Eggs
- 1 Egg White
- 1 Banana, Ripe
- 1 Cup Rolled Oats
- 2 Teaspoons Ground Cinnamon
- 1 Tablespoon Coconut Oil, Divided
- 1 Teaspoon Vanilla Extract, Pure
- ½ Teaspoon Sea Salt

Directions:

- Get out a food processor, grinding your oats until they make a coarse flour.
- Add your cinnamon, egg whites, eggs, banana, vanilla, and salt. Blend until it forms a smooth batter, and then heat a small skillet over medium heat. Heat a half a tablespoon of coconut oil, and then pour your batter in. Cook for two minutes per side, and continue until all of your batter has been used.

Nutrition:
Calories: 306
Protein: 15 Grams
Fat: 15 Grams
Carbs: 17 Grams

Baked French Toast Casserole

Preparation Time: 20 minutes
Cooking Time: 45 minutes
Servings: 12
Ingredients:
1. 1 lb. French bread
2. 1 cup of egg white liquid
3. 6 eggs
4. 1/3 cup maple syrup
5. 1-1/2 cups of rice milk,
6. ½ lb. raspberries
7. ½ lb. blueberries
8. 1 teaspoon of vanilla extract
9. ¾ cup strawberries

Directions:
- Slice the bread into small cubes. Keep them in a greased casserole dish.
- Add all the berries. Only leave a few for the topping.
- Whisk together the egg whites, eggs, rice milk, and maple syrup in a bowl.
- Combine well.
- Put the egg mixture on the top of the bread. Press the bread down. All pieces should be soaked well.
- Add berries on the top. Fill up the holes, if any.
- Refrigerate covered for a couple of hours at least.
- Take out the casserole half an hour before baking.
- Set your oven to 350 degrees F.
- Now, bake your casserole uncovered for 30 minutes.
- Bake for another 15 minutes covered with a foil.
- Let it rest for 15 minutes.
- Serve it warm with maple syrup.

Nutrition:
Calories 200
Carbohydrates 31g
Cholesterol 93mg
Total Fat 4g
Protein 10g

Fiber 2g
Sodium 288mg
Sugar 10g

Whole Grain Blueberry Scones

Preparation Time: 10 minutes
Cooking Time: 25 minutes
Servings: 8
Ingredients:

1. 2 cups of whole-wheat flour
2. ¼ cup maple syrup
3. 6 tablespoons of olive oil
4. 2-1/2 teaspoons baking powder
5. ½ teaspoon sea salt
6. 2 tablespoons of coconut milk
7. 1 teaspoon vanilla extract
8. 1 cup blueberries

Directions:

- Set the oven 400°F. Keep parchment paper on your baking sheet.
- Add the syrup, flour, salt, and baking powder in a bowl. Combine well by whisking together.
- Pour the olive oil into a bowl with the dry ingredients.
- Work the oil into your flour mix.
- Stir the vanilla extract and coconut milk into the dry ingredients bowl.
- Fold in the blueberries gently. Your dough should be sticky and thick.
- Put some flour on your hand then shape the dough into a circle.
- Take a knife and create triangle slices.
- Keep them on the baking sheet. Maintain an 8-inch gap.
- Bake for 25 minutes. Set aside on the baking sheet for cooling once done.

Nutrition:
Calories 331
Carbohydrates 27g
Cholesterol 0mg
Total Fat 23g
Protein 4g
Fiber 4g

Sugar 8g

Spinach Mushroom Omelet

Preparation Time: 3 minutes
Cooking Time: 15 minutes
Servings: 2
Ingredients:

1. 2 tbsp. Olive oil,
2. 1 ½ cup Spinach, fresh, chopped
3. 1 Green onion, diced
4. 3 Eggs
5. 1 oz. Feta cheese
6. 5 Mushrooms, button, sliced
7. ¼ Red onion, diced

Directions:

- Sauté the mushrooms, onions, and spinach for three minutes in one tablespoon of olive oil and set to the side. Beat the eggs well and cook them in the other tablespoon of olive oil for three to four minutes until edges begin to brown. Sprinkle all the other ingredients onto half of the omelet and fold the other half over the sautéed ingredients. Cook for one minute on each side.

Nutrition:
Calories 337
25 grams fat
22 grams protein
5.4 grams carbs
1.3 grams sugar
1 gram fiber

Weekend Breakfast Salad

Preparation Time: 30 minutes
Cooking Time: 0 minutes
Servings: 4
Ingredients:

1. 4 Eggs, hard-boiled
2. 1 Lemon
3. 10 cups Arugula
4. 1 cup Quinoa, cooked and cooled
5. 2 tbsp. Olive oil
6. ½ cup Dill, chopped
7. 1 cup Almonds, chopped
8. 1 Large Avocado, sliced thin
9. ½ cup Cucumber, chopped
10. 1 Large Tomato, cut in wedges

Directions:

- Mix together the quinoa, cucumber, tomatoes, and arugula. Toss these ingredients lightly together with olive oil, salt, and pepper. Divide the salad into 4 plates and arrange the egg and avocado on top. Top each salad with almonds and herbs. Drizzle with juice from the lemon.

Nutrition:
Calories 336
7.7 grams fat
12.3 grams protein
54.6 grams carbs
5.5 grams sugar
5.2 grams fiber

Kale Turmeric Scramble

Preparation Time: 5 minutes
Cooking Time: 10 minutes
Servings: 1
Ingredients:

- 2 tbsp. Olive oil
- ½ cup Kale, shredded
- ½ cup Sprouts
- 1 tbsp. Garlic, minced
- ¼ tsp. Black pepper
- 1 tbsp. Turmeric, ground
- 2 Eggs

Directions:

1. Beat the eggs and add in the turmeric, black pepper, and garlic. Sauté the kale into the olive oil over medium heat for five minutes, and then pour this egg mixture into the pan with the kale. Continue cooking, often stirring, until the eggs are cooked to your preference. Top with raw sprouts and serve.

Nutrition:
Calories 137
8.4 grams fat
7.9 grams carbs
4.8 grams fiber
1.8grams sugar
13.2 grams protein

Poached Salmon Egg Toast

Preparation Time: 10 minutes
Cooking Time: 4 minutes
Servings: 2

- Bread, two slices rye or whole-grain toasted
- ¼ tsp. Lemon juice
- 2 tbs. Avocado, mashed
- ¼ tsp. Black pepper
- 2 Eggs, poached
- 4 oz. Salmon, smoked
- 1 tbsp. Scallions, sliced thin
- 1/8 tsp. Salt

Directions:

- Add lemon juice to avocado with pepper and salt. Spread the mixed avocado over the toasted bread slices. Lay smoked salmon over toast and top with a poached egg. Top with sliced scallions.

Nutrition:

Calories 389
17.2 grams fat
33.5 grams protein
31.5 grams carbs
1.3 grams sugar
9.3 grams fiber

Egg Muffins with Feta and Quinoa

Preparation Time: 15 minutes
Cooking Time: 30 minutes
Servings: 6-12
Ingredients:

- 8 Eggs
- 1 cup Tomatoes, chopped
- ¼ tsp. Salt
- 1 cup Feta cheese
- 1 cup Quinoa, cooked
- 2 tsp. Olive oil
- 1 tbsp. Oregano, fresh chop
- ¼ cup Black olives, chopped
- ¼ cup Onion, chopped

2 cups baby spinach, chopped

Directions:

- Heat oven to 350. Spray oil a muffin pan with twelve cups. Cook spinach, oregano, olives, onion, and tomatoes for five minutes in the olive oil over medium heat. Beat eggs. Add the cooked mix of veggies to the eggs with the cheese and salt. Spoon mix into muffin cups. Bake thirty minutes. These will remain fresh in the fridge for two days. To eat, just wrap in a paper towel and warm in the microwave for thirty seconds.

Nutrition:

Calorie 113
5 grams carbs
6 grams protein
7 grams fat
1-gram sugar

Peaches with Honey Almond Ricotta

Preparation Time: 15 minutes
Cooking Time: 0 minutes
Servings: 4-6
Ingredients:

- Spread
- 1 cup Ricotta, skim milk
- 1 tsp. Honey
- ½ cup Almonds, thin slices
- ¼ cup Almond extract
- To Serve
- ¼ cup Peaches, sliced
- Bread, whole grain bagel or toast

Directions:

Mix the almond extract, honey, ricotta, and almonds. Spread one tablespoon of this mix on toasted bread and cover with peaches.

Nutrition:

Calories 230
9 grams protein
8 grams fat
37 carbs grams
3 fiber grams
34 sugar grams

Quinoa Breakfast Bowl

Preparation Time: 30 minutes
Cooking Time: 0 minutes
Servings: 6
Ingredients:

- 2 cups Quinoa, cooked
- 12 Eggs
- ¼ cup Greek yogurt, plain
- ½ tsp. Salt
- 1 cup Feta cheese
- 1 Pint Cherry tomatoes, cut in halves
- 1 tsp. Black pepper
- 1 tsp. Garlic, minced
- 1 cup Baby spinach, chopped
- 1 tsp. Olive oil

Directions:

- Mix together the eggs, salt, pepper, garlic, onion powder, and yogurt. Cook the spinach and tomatoes for five minutes in the olive oil over medium heat. Pour in the egg mix and stir until eggs have set to your preferred doneness. Mix in quinoa and feta until they are hot. This will store in the fridge for two to three days.

Nutrition:
Calories 340
7.3 grams fat
59.4 grams carbs
6.2 grams fiber
21.4 grams sugar
10.5 grams protein.

Cream Cheese Salmon Toast

Preparation Time: 15 minutes
Cooking Time: 5 minutes
Servings: 2
Ingredients:

- Whole grain or rye toast, two slices
- 1 tbsp. Red onion, chopped fine
- 2 tbsp. Cream cheese, low-fat
- ½ tsp. Basil flakes
- ½ cup Arugula or spinach, chopped
- 2 oz. Smoked salmon

Directions:

- Toast the wheat bread. Mix cream cheese and basil and spread this mixture on the toast. Add salmon, arugula, and onion.

Nutrition:

Calories 291

15.2 grams fat (8.5 saturated)

17.8 grams carbohydrates

3 grams of sugar

Carrot Cake Overnight Oats

Preparation Time: 5 minutes + overnight
Cooking Time: 0 minutes
Servings: 1
Ingredients:
1. 1 cup Coconut or almond milk
2. 1 tbsp. Chia seeds
3. 1 tsp. Cinnamon, ground
4. ½ cup Raisins
5. 2 tbsp. Cream cheese, low fat, at room temperature
6. 1 Large Carrot, peel, and shred
7. 2 tbsp. Honey
8. 1 tsp. Vanilla

Directions:
- Mix together all of the listed ingredients and store them in a safe refrigerator container overnight. Eat cold in the morning. If you choose to warm this, just microwave for one minute and stir well before eating.

Nutrition:
Calories 340
32 grams sugar
8 grams protein
4 grams fat
9 grams fiber
70 grams carbs

Mediterranean Frittata

Preparation Time: 5 minutes
Cooking Time: 20 minutes
Servings: 6
Ingredients:
1. 6 Eggs
2. ¼ cup Feta cheese, crumbled
3. ¼ tsp. Black pepper
4. Oil, spray or olive
5. 1 tsp. Oregano
6. ¼ cup Milk, almond or coconut
7. 1 tsp. Sea salt
8. ¼ cup Black olives, chopped
9. ¼ cup Green olives, chopped
10. ¼ cup Tomatoes, diced

Directions:
- Heat oven to 400. Oil one eight by eight-inch baking dish. Beat the milk into the eggs, and then add other ingredients. Pour all of this mixture into the baking dish and bake for twenty minutes.

Nutrition: Calories 107
2 grams sugars
7 fat grams
3 carb grams
7 grams protein

Maple Oatmeal

Preparation Time: 5 minutes
Cooking Time: 20 minutes
Servings: 4
Ingredients:
1. 1 tsp. Maple flavoring
2. 1 tsp. Cinnamon
3. 3 tbsp. Sunflower seeds
4. ½ cup Pecans, chopped
5. ¼ cup Coconut flakes, unsweetened
6. ½ cup Walnuts, chopped
7. ½ cup Milk, almond or coconut
8. 4 tbsp. Chia seeds

Directions:
- Pulse the sunflower seeds, walnuts, and pecans in a food processor to crumble. Or you can just put the nuts in a sturdy plastic bag, wrap the bag with a towel, lay it on a sturdy surface, and beat the towel with a hammer until the nuts are crumbled. Mix the crushed nuts with the rest of the ingredients and pour them into a large pot. Simmer this mixture over low heat for thirty minutes. Stir often, so the mix does not stick to the bottom. Serve garnished with fresh fruit or a sprinkle of cinnamon if desired.

Nutrition:
Calories 374
3.2 grams carbs
9.25 grams protein
34.59 grams fat

Tomato Omelet

Preparation Time: 2 minutes
Cooking Time: 8 minutes
Servings: 1
Ingredients:
1. 2 Eggs
2. ½ cup Basil, fresh
3. ½ cup Cherry tomatoes
4. 1 tsp. Black pepper
5. ¼ cup Cheese, any type, shredded
6. ½ tsp. Salt
7. 2 tbsp. Olive oil

Directions:
- Cut the tomatoes into quarters. Fry the tomatoes for 3 hours. Set the tomatoes off to the side. Add the salt and pepper to the eggs in a small bowl and beat together well. Pour the mix of beaten egg into the pan and use a spatula to gently work around the edges under the omelet, letting the eggs fry unmoved for three minutes. When just the center third of the egg mix is still runny, add on the basil, tomatoes, and cheese. Fold over half of the omelet onto the other half. Cook two more minutes and serve.

Nutrition:
Calories 342
8 grams carbs
20 grams protein
25.3 grams fat

Tuna & Sweet Potato Croquettes

Preparation Time: 15 minutes
Cooking Time: 12 minutes
Servings: 8
Ingredients:
1. 1 tablespoon coconut oil
2. ½ large onion, chopped
3. 1 (1-inch piece fresh ginger, minced
4. 3 garlic cloves, minced
5. 1 Serrano pepper, seeded and minced
6. ½ teaspoon ground coriander
7. ¼ teaspoon ground turmeric
8. ¼ teaspoon red chili powder
9. ¼ teaspoon garam masala
10. Salt, to taste
11. Freshly ground black pepper, to taste
12. 2 (5 oz.) cans tuna
13. 1 cup sweet potato, peeled and mashed
14. 1 egg
15. ¼ cup tapioca flour
16. ¼ cup almond flour
17. Olive oil, as required

Directions:
- In a frying pan, warm the coconut oil on medium heat.
- Put onion, ginger, garlic, and Serrano pepper and sauté for approximately 5-6 minutes.
- Stir in spices and sauté approximately 1 minute more.
- Transfer the onion mixture in a bowl.
- Add tuna and sweet potato and mix till well combined.
- Make equal sized oblong shaped patties in the mixture.
- Arrange the croquettes inside a baking sheet in a very single layer and refrigerate for overnight.
- In a shallow dish, beat the egg.
- In another shallow dish, mix together both flours.
- In a big skillet, heat the enough oil.
- Add croquettes in batches and shallow fry for around 2-3 minutes per side.

Nutrition:
Calories: 404
Fat: 9g
Carbohydrates: 20g
Fiber: 4g
Protein: 30g

Quinoa & Veggie Croquettes

Preparation Time: 15 minutes
Cooking Time: 9 minutes
Servings: 12-15
Ingredients:

- 1 tbsp. essential olive oil
- ½ cup frozen peas, thawed
- 2 minced garlic cloves
- 1 cup cooked quinoa
- 2 large boiled potatoes, peeled and mashed
- ¼ cup fresh cilantro leaves, chopped
- 2 teaspoons ground cumin
- 1 teaspoon garam masala
- ¼ teaspoon ground turmeric
- Salt, to taste
- Freshly ground black pepper, to taste
- Olive oil, for frying

Directions:

1. In a frying pan, warm oil on medium heat.
2. Add peas and garlic and sauté for about 1 minute.
3. Transfer the pea mixture into a large bowl.
4. Add the remainder ingredients and mix till well combined.
5. Make equal sized oblong shaped patties from your mixture.
6. In a huge skillet, heat oil on medium-high heat.
7. Add croquettes and fry for about 4 minutes per side.

Nutrition:
Calories: 367
Fat: 6g
Carbohydrates: 17g
Fiber: 5g
Protein: 22g

Turkey Burgers

Preparation Time: 15 minutes
Cooking Time: 8 minutes
Servings: 5
Ingredients:

- 1 ripe pear, peeled, cored and chopped roughly
- 1-pound lean ground turkey
- 1 teaspoon fresh ginger, grated finely
- 2 minced garlic cloves
- 1 teaspoon fresh rosemary, minced
- 1 teaspoon fresh sage, minced
- Salt, to taste
- Freshly ground black pepper, to taste
- 1-2 tablespoons coconut oil

Directions:

- In a blender, add pear and pulse till smooth.
- Transfer the pear mixture in a large bowl with remaining ingredients except for oil and mix till well combined.
- Make small equal sized 10 patties from the mixture.
- In a heavy-bottomed frying pan, heat oil on medium heat.
- Add the patties and cook for around 4-5 minutes.
- Flip the inside and cook for approximately 2-3 minutes.

Nutrition:
Calories: 477
Fat: 15g
Carbohydrates: 26g
Fiber: 11g
Protein: 35g

Salmon Burgers

Preparation Time: 15 minutes
Cooking Time: 8 minutes
Servings: 3
Ingredients:

1. 1 (6-oz. can) skinless, boneless salmon, drained
2. 1 celery rib, chopped
3. ½ of a medium onion, chopped
4. 2 large eggs
5. 1 tablespoon plus 1 teaspoon coconut flour
6. 1 tablespoon dried dill, crushed
7. 1 teaspoon lemon
8. Salt, to taste
9. Freshly ground black pepper, to taste
10. 3 tablespoons coconut oil

Directions:

- In a substantial bowl, add salmon and which has a fork, break it into small pieces.
- Add remaining ingredients excluding the for oil and mix till well combined.
- Make 6 equal sized small patties from the mixture.
- In a substantial skillet, melt coconut oil on medium-high heat.
- Cook the patties for around 3-4 minutes per side.

Nutrition:
Calories: 393
Fat: 12g
Carbohydrates: 19g
Fiber: 5g
Protein: 24g

Preparation Time: 15 minutes
Cooking Time: 55 minutes
Servings: 12
Ingredients:

1. ½ cup dry quinoa
2. 1½ cups water
3. 1 cup cooked corn kernels
4. 1 (15 oz.) can black beans, drained
5. 1 small boiled potato, peeled
6. 1 small onion, chopped
7. ½ teaspoon fresh ginger, grated finely
8. 1 teaspoon garlic, minced
9. ½ cup fresh cilantro, chopped
10. 1 teaspoon flax meal
11. 1 teaspoon ground cumin
12. 1 teaspoon paprika
13. 1 teaspoon chili flakes
14. ½ teaspoon ground turmeric
15. Salt, to taste
16. Freshly ground black pepper, to taste

Directions:

- In a pan, add water and quinoa on high heat and provide to a boil.
- Lower the heat to medium and simmer for around 15-twenty or so minutes.
- Drain excess water.
- Set the oven to 375°F. Line a sizable baking sheet that has a parchment paper.
- In a sizable bowl, add quinoa and remaining ingredients.
- With a fork, mix till well combined.
- Make equal-sized patties from the mixture.
- Arrange the patties onto the prepared baking sheet in the single layer.
- Bake for around 20-25 minutes.
- Carefully, alter the side and cook for about 8-10 minutes.

Nutrition:
Calories: 400
Fat: 9g

Carbohydrates: 27g
Fiber: 12g
Protein: 38g

Veggie Balls

Preparation Time: 15 minutes
Cooking Time: 25 minutes
Servings: 5-6
Ingredients:
1. 2 medium sweet potatoes, cubed into ½-inch size
2. 2 tablespoons coconut milk
3. 1 cup fresh kale leaves, trimmed and chopped
4. 1 medium shallot, chopped finely
5. 1 tsp. ground cumin
6. ½ teaspoon granulated garlic
7. ¼ tsp. ground turmeric
8. Salt, to taste
9. Freshly ground black pepper, to taste

Ground flax seeds, as required

Directions:
- Set the oven to 400°F. Line a baking sheet with parchment paper.
- In a pan of water, arrange a steamer basket.
- Bring the sweet potato in a steamer basket and steam approximately 10-15 minutes.
- In a sizable bowl, put the sweet potato.
- Add coconut milk and mash well.
- Add remaining ingredients except for flax seeds and mix till well combined.
- Make about 1½-2-inch balls from your mixture.
- Arrange the balls onto the prepared baking sheet inside a single layer.
- Sprinkle with flax seeds.
- Bake for around 20-25 minutes.

Nutrition:
Calories: 464
Fat: 12g
Carbohydrates: 20g
 Fiber: 8g
Protein: 27g

Coconut & Banana Cookies

Preparation Time: 15 minutes
Cooking Time: 25 minutes
Servings: 7
Ingredients:
1. 2 cups unsweetened coconut, shredded
2. 3 medium bananas, peeled
3. ½ tsp. ground cinnamon
4. ½ tsp. ground turmeric
5. Pinch of salt, to taste
6. Freshly ground black pepper

Directions:
- Set the oven to 350°F. Line a cookie sheet a lightly greased parchment paper.
- In a mixer, put all together ingredients and pulse till a dough-like mixture forms.
- Form small balls through the mixture and set onto a prepared cookie sheet in a single layer.
- Using your fingers, press along the balls to create the cookies.
- Bake for at least 15-20 minutes or till golden brown.

Nutrition:
Calories: 370
Fat: 4g
Carbohydrates: 28g
Fiber: 11g
Protein: 33g

Fennel Seeds Cookies

Preparation Time: 10 minutes
Cooking Time: 20 minutes
Servings: 5
Ingredients:
1. 1/3 cup coconut flour
2. ¼ teaspoon whole fennel seeds
3. ½ teaspoon fresh ginger, grated finely
4. ¼ cup coconut oil, softened
5. 2 tablespoons raw honey
6. 1 teaspoon vanilla extract
7. Pinch of ground cinnamon
8. Pinch of salt
9. Pinch freshly ground black pepper

Directions:
- Set the oven to 360°F. Line a cookie sheet that has a parchment paper.
- In a substantial bowl, add all together the ingredients and mix till an even dough form.
- Form a small balls in the mixture make onto a prepared cookie sheet inside a single layer.
- Using your fingers, gently press along the balls to create the cookies.
- Bake for at least 9 minutes or till golden brown.

Nutrition:
Calories: 353
Fat: 5g
Carbohydrates: 19g
Fiber: 3g
Protein: 25g

Almond Scones

Preparation Time: 10 minutes
Cooking Time: 20 minutes
Servings: 6
Ingredients:
1. 1 cup almonds
2. 1 1/3 cups almond flour
3. ¼ cup arrowroot flour
4. 1 tablespoon coconut flour
5. 1 teaspoon ground turmeric
6. Salt, to taste
7. Freshly ground black pepper, to taste
8. 1 egg
9. ¼ cup essential olive oil
10. 3 tablespoons raw honey
11. 1 teaspoon vanilla flavoring

Directions:
- In a mixer, put almonds then pulse till chopped roughly
- Move the chopped almonds in a big bowl.
- Put flours and spices and mix well.
- In another bowl, put the remaining ingredients and beat till well combined.
- Put the flour mixture into the egg mixture then mix till well combined.
- Arrange a plastic wrap over the cutting board.
- Place the dough over the cutting board.
- Using both of your hands, pat into 1-inch thick circle.
- Cut the circle in 6 wedges.
- Set the scones onto a cookie sheet in a single layer.
- Bake for at least 15-20 minutes.

Nutrition:
Calories: 304
Fat: 3g

Carbohydrates: 22g
 Fiber: 6g
Protein: 20g

Oven-Poached Eggs

Preparation Time: 2minutes
Cooking Time: 11minutes
Servings: 4
Ingredients:

- 6 eggs, at room temperature
- Water
- Ice bath
- 2 cups water, chilled
- 2 cups of ice cubes

Directions:

1. Set the oven to 350°F. Put 2 cups of water into a deep roasting tin, and place it into the lowest rack of the oven.
2. Place one egg into each cup of cupcake/muffin tins, along with one tablespoon of water.
3. Carefully place muffin tins into the middle rack of the oven.
4. Bake eggs for 45 minutes.
5. Turn off the heat immediately. Take off the muffin tins from the oven and set on a cake rack to cool before extracting eggs.
6. Pour ice bath ingredients into a large heat-resistant bowl.
7. Bring the eggs into an ice bath to stop the cooking process. After 10 minutes, drain eggs well. Use as needed.

Nutrition:
Calories: 357 kcal
Protein: 17.14 g
Fat: 24.36 g
Carbohydrates: 16.19 g

Cranberry and Raisins Granola

Preparation Time: 15 minutes
Cooking Time: 20 minutes
Servings: 4
Ingredients:
1. 4 cups old-fashioned rolled oats
2. 1/4 cup sesame seeds
3. 1 cup dried cranberries
4. 1 cup golden raisins
5. 1/8 teaspoon nutmeg
6. 2 tablespoons olive oil
7. 1/2 cup almonds, slivered
8. 2 tablespoons warm water
9. 1 teaspoon vanilla extract
10. 1 teaspoon cinnamon
11. 1/4 teaspoon of salt
12. 6 tablespoons maple syrup
13. 1/3 cup of honey

Directions:
1. In a bowl, mix the sesame seeds, nutmeg, almonds, oats, salt, and cinnamon.
2. In another bowl, mix the oil, water, vanilla, honey, and syrup. Gradually pour the mixture into the oats mixture. Toss to combine. Spread the mixture into a greased jelly-roll pan. Bake in the oven at 300°F for at least 55 minutes. Stir and break the clumps every 10 minutes.
3. Once you get it from the oven, stir the cranberries and raisins. Allow cooling. This will last for a week when stored in an airtight container and up to a month when stored in the fridge.

Nutrition:
Calories: 698 kcal
Protein: 21.34 g
Fat: 20.99 g
Carbohydrates: 148.59 g

Spicy Marble Eggs

Preparation Time: 15 minutes
Cooking Time: 2 hours
Servings: 12
Ingredients:

- 6 medium-boiled eggs, unpeeled, cooled
- For the Marinade
- 2 oolong black tea bags
- 3 Tbsp. brown sugar
- 1 thumb-sized fresh ginger, unpeeled, crushed
- 3 dried star anise, whole
- 2 dried bay leaves
- 3 Tbsp. light soy sauce
- 4 Tbsp. dark soy sauce
- 4 cups of water
- 1 dried cinnamon stick, whole
- 1 tsp. salt
- 1 tsp. dried Szechuan peppercorns

Directions:

- Using the back of a metal spoon, crack eggshells in places to create a spider web effect. Do not peel. Set aside until needed.
- Pour marinade into large Dutch oven set over high heat. Put lid partially on. Bring water to a rolling boil, about 5 minutes. Turn off heat.
- Secure lid. Steep ingredients for 10 minutes.
- Using a slotted spoon, fish out and discard solids. Cool marinade completely to room proceeding.
- Place eggs into an airtight non-reactive container just small enough to snugly fit all these in.
- Pour in marinade. Eggs should be completely submerged in liquid. Discard leftover marinade, if any. Line container rim with generous layers of saran wrap. Secure container lid.
- Chill eggs for 24 hours before using.
- Extract eggs and drain each piece well before using, but keep the rest submerged in the marinade.

Nutrition:

Calories: 75 kcal
Protein: 4.05 g
Fat: 4.36 g
Carbohydrates: 4.83 g

Nutty Oats Pudding

Preparation Time: 5 minutes
Cooking Time: 0 minutes
Servings: 3 -5
Ingredients:
1. ¼ cup rolled oats
2. 1 tablespoon yogurt, fat-free
3. 1 ½ tablespoon natural peanut butter
4. ¼ cup dry milk
5. 1 teaspoon peanuts, finely chopped
6. ½ cup of water

Directions:
- Using a microwaveable-safe bowl, put together peanut butter and dry milk. Whisk well. Add in water to achieve a smooth consistency. Add in oats.
- Cover bowl with plastic wrap. Create a small hole for the steam to escape.
- Place inside the microwave oven for 1 minute on high powder.
- Continue heating, this time on medium power for 90 seconds. Let sit for 5 minutes.
- To serve, spoon an equal amount of cereals in a bowl top with peanuts and yogurt.

Nutrition:
Calories: 70 kcal
Protein: 4.25 g
Fat: 3.83 g
Carbohydrates: 6.78 g

Almond Pancakes with Coconut Flakes

Preparation: Time: 5 minutes
Cooking Time: 10 minutes
Servings: 6
Ingredients:
1. 1 overripe banana, mashed
2. 2 eggs, yolks, and whites separated
3. ½ cup unsweetened applesauce
4. 1 cup almond flour, finely milled
5. ¼ cup of water
6. ¼ tsp. coconut oil
7. Garnish
8. 2 Tbsp. blanched almond flakes
9. Dash of cinnamon powder
10. ¼ cup coconut flakes, sweetened
11. Pinch of sea salt
12. Pure maple syrup, use sparingly

Directions:
- Whisk egg whites until soft peaks form.
- Except for egg whites and coconut oil, combine remaining ingredients in another bowl. Mix until batter comes together.
- Gently fold in egg whites. Make sure that you don't over mix, or the pancake will become dense and chewy.
- Pour oil into a nonstick skillet set over medium heat.
- Wait for the oil to heat up before dropping in approximately ½ cup of batter. Cook until each side are set, and bubbles form in the center. Turn on the other side then cook for another 2 minutes.
- Transfer flapjacks to a plate. Repeat step until all batter is cooked. Pour in more oil into the skillet only if needed. This recipe should yield between 4 to 6 medium-sized pancakes.
- Stack pancakes. Pour the desired amount of pure maple syrup on top. Garnish each stack with cinnamon-flavored almond-coconut flakes just before serving.
- For the garnish, set the oven to 350°F for at least 10 minutes before use. Line a baking sheet with parchment paper. Set aside.

- Mix almond and coconut flakes together in a bowl. Spread mixture evenly on a prepared baking sheet.
- Bake for 7 to 10 minutes until flakes turn golden brown. Stir almond and coconut flakes once midway through roasting to prevent over-browning.
- Remove the baking sheet from the oven. Cool almond and coconut flakes for at least 10 minutes before sprinkling in cinnamon powder and salt. Toss to combine. Set aside.

Nutrition:
Calories: 62 kcal
Protein: 2.24 g
Fat: 4.01 g
Carbohydrates: 4.46 g

Bake Apple Turnover

Preparation Time: 30 minutes
Cooking Time: 25 minutes
Servings: 4
Ingredients:
1. For the turnovers
2. 4 apples, peeled, cored, diced into bite-sized pieces
3. 1 Tbsp. almond flour
4. All-purpose flour, for rolling out the dough
5. 1 frozen puff pastry, thawed
6. ½ cup palm sugar, crumbled by hand to loosen granules
7. ½ tsp. cinnamon powder
8. For the egg wash
9. 1 egg white, whisked in
10. 2 Tbsp. water

Directions:
- For the filling: combine almond flour, cinnamon powder, and palm sugar until these resemble coarse meal. Toss in diced apples until well coated. Set aside.
- On a lightly floured surface, roll the puff pastry until ¼ inch thin. Slice into 8 pieces of 4" x 4" squares.
- Divide prepared apples into 8 equal portions. Spoon on individual puff pastry squares. Fold in half diagonally. Press edges to seal.
- Place each filled pastry on a baking tray lined with parchment paper. Make sure there is ample space between pastries.
- Freeze for at least 20 minutes, or till ready to bake.
- Preheat oven to 400°F or 205°C for at 10 minutes.
- Brush frozen pastries with egg wash. Bring in a hot oven, and cook for 12 to 15 minutes, or until these turn golden brown all over.
- Take off the baking tray in the oven immediately. Cool slightly for easier handling.
- Place 1 apple turnover on a plate. Serve warm.

Nutrition:
Calories: 203 kcal
Protein: 5.29 g

Fat: 4.4 g
Carbohydrates: 38.25 g

Quinoa and Cauliflower Congee

Preparation Time: 10 minutes
Cooking Time: 1 hour
Servings: 8
Ingredients:

- 1 cauliflower head, minced
- 2 tablespoons red quinoa
- 2 leeks, minced
- 1 tablespoon fresh ginger, grated
- 2 garlic cloves, grated
- 6 cups of water
- 2 tablespoons brown rice
- 1 tablespoon olive oil
- 1 tablespoon fish sauce
- 2 onions, minced
- Pinch of white pepper
- For Garnish
- 4 eggs, soft-boiled
- 2 red chili, minced
- 1 lime, sliced into wedges
- ¼ cup packed basil leaves, torn
- ¼ cup loosely packed cilantro leaves, torn
- ¼ cup loosely packed spearmint leaves, torn

Directions:

1. Put olive oil into a huge skillet on medium heat. Sauté shallots, garlic, and ginger until limp and aromatic; pour into a slow cooker set at medium heat.
2. Except for garnishes, pour remaining ingredients into slow cooker; stir. Put the lid on. Cook for 6 hours. Turn off heat. Taste; adjust seasoning if needed.
3. Ladle congee into individual bowls. Garnish with basil leaves, cilantro leaves, red chilli, and spearmint leaves. Add 1 piece of soft-boiled egg on top of each; serve with a wedge of lime on the side. Slice egg just before eating so yolk runs into congee. Squeeze lime juice into congee just before eating.

Nutrition:

Calories: 138 kcal
Protein: 7.23 g
Fat: 7.65 g
Carbohydrates: 10.76 g

Breakfast Arrozcaldo

Preparation Time: 20 minutes
Cooking Time: 30 minutes
Servings: 5
Ingredients:
1. 6 eggs, white only
2. 1½ cups brown rice, cooked
3. For the filling
4. ¼ cup raisins
5. ½ cup frozen peas, thawed
6. 1 white onion, minced
7. 1 garlic clove, minced
8. oil, for greasing

Directions:
1. For the filling, spray a small amount of oil into a skillet set over medium heat. Add in onion and garlic. Stir-fry until former is limp and transparent.
2. Stir-fry while breaking up clumps, about 2 minutes. Add in remaining ingredients. Stir-fry for another minute.
3. Turn down the heat, and let filling cook for 10 to 15 minutes, or until juices are greatly reduced. Stir often. Turn off heat. Divide into 6 equal portions.
4. For the eggs, spray a small amount of oil into a smaller skillet set over medium heat. Cook eggs. Discard yolk. Transfer to holding the plate.
5. To serve, place 1 portion of rice on a plate, 1 portion of filling, and 1 egg white. Serve warm.

Nutrition:
Calories: 53 kcal
Protein: 6.28 g
Fat: 1.35 g
Carbohydrates: 3.59 g

Apple Bruschetta with Almonds and Blackberries

Preparation Time: 20 minutes
Cooking Time: 30 minutes
Servings: 5
Ingredients:
- 1 apple, sliced into ¼-inch thick half-moons
- ¼ cup blackberries, thawed, lightly mashed
- ½ tsp. fresh lemon juice
- 1/8 cup almond slivers, toasted
- Sea salt

Directions:
- Drizzle lemon juice on apple slices. Put these on a tray lined with parchment paper.
- Spread a small number of mashed berries on top of each slice. Top these off with the desired amount of almond slivers.
- Sprinkle sea salt on "bruschetta" just before serving.

Nutrition:
Calories: 56 kcal
Protein: 1.53 g
Fat: 1.43 g
Carbohydrates: 9.87 g

Hash Browns

Preparation Time: 15 minutes
Cooking Time: 15 minutes
Servings: 4
Ingredients:
1. 1 pound Russet potatoes, peeled, processed using a grater
2. Pinch of sea salt
3. Pinch of black pepper, to taste
4. 3 Tbsp. olive oil

Directions:
- Line a microwave safe-dish with paper towels. Spread shredded potatoes on top. Microwave veggies on the highest heat setting for 2 minutes. Remove from heat.
- Pour 1 tablespoon of oil into a non-stick skillet set over medium heat.
- Cooking in batches, place a generous pinch of potatoes into the hot oil. Press down using the back of a spatula.
- Cook for 3 minutes every side, or until brown and crispy. Drain on paper towels. Repeat step for remaining potatoes. Add more oil as needed.
- Season with salt and pepper. Serve.

Nutrition:
Calories:
200 kcal
Protein: 4.03 g
Fat: 11.73 g
Carbohydrates: 20.49 g

Sun-Dried Tomato Garlic Bruschetta

Preparation Time: 10 minutes
Cooking Time: 5 minutes
Servings: 6
Ingredients:
1. 2 slices sourdough bread, toasted
2. 1 tsp. chives, minced
3. 1 garlic clove, peeled
4. 2 tsp. sun-dried tomatoes in olive oil, minced
5. 1 tsp. olive oil

Directions:
- Vigorously rub garlic clove on 1 side of each of the toasted bread slices
- Spread equal portions of sun-dried tomatoes on the garlic side of bread. Sprinkle chives and drizzle olive oil on top.
- Pop both slices into oven toaster, and cook until well heated through.
- Place bruschetta on a plate. Serve warm.

Nutrition:
Calories: 149 kcal
Protein: 6.12 g
Fat: 2.99 g
Carbohydrates: 24.39 g

Mushroom Crêpes

Preparation Time: 1 hour 30 minutes
Cooking Time: 30 minutes
Servings: 6
Ingredients:
1. 2 eggs
2. 3/4 cup milk
3. 1/2 cup all-purpose flour
4. 1/4 teaspoon salt
5. For the filling
6. 3 tablespoons all-purpose flour
7. 2 cups of cremini mushrooms, sliced
8. 3/4 cup chicken broth
9. 1/2 cup Parmesan cheese, grated
10. 1/8 teaspoon cayenne
11. 1/8 teaspoon nutmeg
12. ¾ cup milk
13. 3 garlic cloves, minced
14. 2 tablespoons of parsley (chopped)
15. 6 slices of deli-sliced cooked lean ham
16. 1/4 teaspoon of salt
17. Freshly ground pepper

Directions:
- Put and combine the salt and flour in a bowl. In another bowl, whisk the eggs and milk. Gradually combine the two mixtures until smooth. Leave for 15 minutes.
- Spray a skillet using non-stick cooking spray and put over medium heat. Stir the batter a little. Add 1/4 of the batter into the skillet. Tilt the skillet to form a thin and even crêpe. Cook for 1-2 minutes or until the bottom is golden and the top is set. Flip and cook for 20 seconds. Transfer to a plate.
- Repeat the steps with the remaining batter. Loosely cover the cooked crêpes with plastic wrap.
- For the filling. Put all together the ingredients for filling in a saucepan on medium heat – flour, milk, cayenne, nutmeg, and pepper. Constantly whisk until thick or around 7 minutes. Remove from the stove. Stir in a tablespoon of parsley and cheese. Loosely cover to keep warm.

- Spray a skillet using non-stick cooking spray and put over medium heat. Cook the garlic and mushrooms. Season with salt. Cook for 6 minutes or until the mushrooms are soft. Add 2 tablespoons of sherry. Cook for a couple of minutes. Remove from the stove. Add the remaining parsley and stir.
- Put the crêpes side by side on a flat surface. Spread a tablespoon of the sauce and 2 tablespoons of the cooked mushrooms. Roll up the crêpes and transfer them to a greased baking dish. Put all the sauce on top. Bake in the oven at 450°F for 15 minutes.

Nutrition:
Calories: 232 kcal
Protein: 16.51 g
Fat: 10.8 g
Carbohydrates: 16.25 g

Oat Porridge with Cherry & Coconut

Preparation Time: 10 minutes
Cooking Time: 0 minutes
Servings: 3
Ingredients:
1. 1 ½ cups regular oats
2. 3 cups coconut milk
3. 4 tbsp. chia seed
4. 3 tbsp. raw cacao
5. Coconut shavings
6. Dark chocolate shavings
7. Fresh or frozen tart cherries
8. A pinch of stevia, optional
9. Maple syrup, to taste (optional)

Directions:
- Combine the oats, milk, stevia, and cacao in a medium saucepan over medium heat and bring to a boil. Lower the heat, then simmer until the oats are cooked to desired doneness.
- Divide the porridge among 3 serving bowls and top with dark chocolate and coconut shavings, cherries, and a little drizzle of maple syrup.

Nutrition:
Calories: 343 kcal
Protein: 15.64 g
Fat: 12.78 g
Carbohydrates: 41.63 g

Gingerbread Oatmeal Breakfast

Preparation Time: 10 minutes
Cooking Time: 0 minutes
Servings: 4
Ingredients:
1. 1 cup steel-cut oats
2. 4 cups drinking water
3. Organic Maple syrup, to taste
4. 1 tsp ground cloves
5. 1 ½ tbsp. ground cinnamon
6. 1/8 tsp nutmeg
7. ¼ tsp ground ginger
8. ¼ tsp ground coriander
9. ¼ tsp ground allspice
10. ¼ tsp ground cardamom
11. Fresh mixed berries

Directions:
- Cook the oats based on the package instructions. When it comes to a boil, reduce heat and simmer.
- Stir in all the spices and continue cooking until cooked to desired doneness.
- Serve in four serving bowls and drizzle with maple syrup and top with fresh berries.
- Enjoy!

Nutrition:
Calories: 87 kcal
Protein: 5.82 g
Fat: 3.26 g
Carbohydrates: 18.22 g

Apple, Ginger, and Rhubarb Muffins

Preparation Time: 15 minutes
Cooking Time: 25 minutes
Servings: 4
Ingredients:
1. ½ cup finely ground almonds
2. ¼ cup brown rice flour
3. ½ cup buckwheat flour
4. 1/8 cup unrefined raw sugar
5. 2 tbsp. arrowroot flour
6. 1 tbsp. linseed meal
7. 2 tbsp. crystallized ginger, finely chopped
8. ½ tsp. ground ginger
9. ½ tsp. ground cinnamon
10. 2 tsp. gluten-free baking powder
11. A pinch of fine sea salt
12. 1 small apple, peeled and finely diced
13. 1 cup finely chopped rhubarb
14. 1/3 cup almond/ rice milk
15. 1 large egg
16. ¼ cup extra virgin olive oil
17. 1 tsp. pure vanilla extract

Directions:
- Set your oven to 350Fgrease an eight-cup muffin tin and line with paper cases.
- Combine the almond four, linseed meal, ginger and sugar in a mixing bowl. Sieve this mixture over the other flours, spices and baking powder and use a whisk to combine well.
- Stir in the apple and rhubarb in the flour mixture until evenly coated.
- In a separate bowl, whisk the milk, vanilla, and egg then pour it into the dry mixture. Stir until just combined – don't overwork the batter as this can yield very tough muffins.
- Scoop the mixture into the arrange muffin tin and top with a few slices of rhubarb. Bake for at least 25 minutes, till they start turning golden or when an inserted toothpick emerges clean.
- Take off from the oven and let sit for at least 5 minutes before transferring the muffins to a wire rack for further cooling.

- Serve warm with a glass of squeezed juice.
- Enjoy!

Nutrition:
Calories: 325 kcal
Protein: 6.32 g
Fat: 9.82 g
Carbohydrates: 55.71 g

Anti-Inflammatory Breakfast Frittata

Preparation Time: 10 minutes
Cooking Time: 40 minutes
Servings: 4
Ingredients:
1. 4 large eggs
2. 6 egg whites
3. 450g button mushrooms
4. 450g baby spinach
5. 125g firm tofu
6. 1 onion, chopped
7. 1 tbsp. minced garlic
8. ½ tsp. ground turmeric
9. ½ tsp. cracked black pepper
10. ¼ cup water
11. Kosher salt to taste

Directions:
- Set your oven to 350F.
- Sauté the mushrooms in a little bit of extra virgin olive oil in a large non-stick ovenproof pan over medium heat. Add the onions once the mushrooms start turning golden and cook for 3 minutes until the onions become soft.
- Stir in the garlic then cook for at least 30 seconds until fragrant before adding the spinach. Pour in water, cover, and cook until the spinach becomes wilted for about 2 minutes.
- Take off the lid and continue cooking up to the water evaporates. Now, combine the eggs, egg whites, tofu, pepper, turmeric, and salt in a bowl. When all the liquid has evaporated, pour in the egg mixture, let cook for about 2 minutes until the edges start setting, then transfer to the oven and bake for about 25 minutes or until cooked.
- Take off from the oven then let sit for at least 5 minutes before cutting it into quarters and serving.
- Enjoy!
- Baby spinach and mushrooms boost the nutrient profile of the eggs to provide you with amazing anti-inflammatory benefits.

Nutrition:
Calories: 521 kcal

Protein: 29.13 g
Fat: 10.45 g
Carbohydrates: 94.94 g

Breakfast Sausage and Mushroom Casserole

Preparation Time: 20 minutes
Cooking Time: 45 minutes
Servings: 4
Ingredients:
1. 450g of Italian sausage, cooked and crumbled
2. Three-fourth cup of coconut milk
3. 8 ounces of white mushrooms, sliced
4. 1 medium onion, finely diced
5. 2 Tablespoons of organic ghee
6. 6 free-range eggs
7. 600g of sweet potatoes
8. 1 red bell pepper, roasted
9. 3/4 tsp. of ground black pepper, divided
10. 1 ½ tsp. of sea salt, divided

Directions:
- Peel and shred the sweet potatoes.
- Take a bowl, fill it with ice-cold water, and soak the sweet potatoes in it. Set aside.
- Peel the roasted bell pepper, remove its seeds and finely dice it.
- Set the oven 375°F.
- Get a casserole baking dish and grease it with the organic ghee.
- Put a skillet over medium flame and cook the mushrooms in it. Cook until the mushrooms are crispy and brown.
- Take the mushrooms out and mix them with the crumbled sausage.
- Now sauté the onions in the same skillet. Cook up to the onions are soft and golden. This should take about 4 – 5 minutes.
- Take the onions out and mix them in the sausage-mushroom mixture.
- Add the diced bell pepper to the same mixture.
- Mix well and set aside for a while.
- Now drain the soaked shredded potatoes, put them on a paper towel, and pat dry.

- Bring the sweet potatoes in a bowl and add about a teaspoon of salt and half a teaspoon of ground black pepper to it. Mix well and set aside.
- Now take a large bowl and crack the eggs in it.
- Break the eggs and then blend in the coconut milk.
- Stir in the remaining black pepper and salt.
- Take the greased casserole dish and spread the seasoned sweet potatoes evenly in the base of the dish.
- Next, spread the sausage mixture evenly in the dish.
- Finally, spread the egg mixture.
- Now cover the casserole dish using a piece of aluminum foil.
- Bake for 20 - 30 minutes. To check if the casserole is baked properly, insert a tester in the middle of the casserole, and it should come out clean.
- Uncover the casserole dish and bake it again, uncovered for 5 - 10 minutes, until the casserole is a little golden on the top.
- Allow it to cool for 10 minutes.
- Enjoy!

Nutrition:

Calories: 598 kcal

Protein: 28.65 g

Fat: 36.75 g

Carbohydrates: 48.01 g

Yummy Steak Muffins

Preparation Time: 10 minutes
Cooking Time: 20 minutes
Servings: 4
Ingredients:
1. 1 cup red bell pepper, diced
2. 2 Tablespoons of water
3. 8 ounce thin steak, cooked and finely chopped
4. ¼ teaspoon of sea salt
5. Dash of freshly ground black pepper
6. 8 free-range eggs
7. 1 cup of finely diced onion

Directions:
- Set the oven to 350°F
- Take 8 muffin tins and line then with parchment paper liners.
- Get a large bowl and crack all the eggs in it.
- Beat well the eggs.
- Blend in all the remaining ingredients.
- Spoon the batter into the arrange muffin tins. Fill three-fourth of each tin.
- Put the muffin tins in the preheated oven for about 20 minutes, until the muffins are baked and set in the middle.
- Enjoy!

Nutrition:
Calories: 151 kcal
Protein: 17.92 g
Fat: 7.32 g
Carbohydrates: 3.75 g

White and Green Quiche

Preparation Time: 10 minutes
Cooking Time: 40 minutes
Servings: 3
Ingredients:
1. 3 cups of fresh spinach, chopped
2. 15 large free-range eggs
3. 3 cloves of garlic, minced
4. 5 white mushrooms, sliced
5. 1 small sized onion, finely chopped
6. 1 ½ teaspoon of baking powder
7. Ground black pepper to taste
8. 1 ½ cups of coconut milk
9. Ghee, as required to grease the dish
10. Sea salt to taste

Directions:
- Set the oven to 350°F.
- Get a baking dish then grease it with the organic ghee.
- Break all the eggs in a huge bowl then whisk well.
- Stir in coconut milk. Beat well
- While you are whisking the eggs, start adding the remaining ingredients in it.
- When all the ingredients are thoroughly blended, pour all of it into the prepared baking dish.
- Bake for at least 40 minutes, up to the quiche is set in the middle.
- Enjoy!

Nutrition:
Calories: 608 kcal
Protein: 20.28 g
Fat: 53.42 g
Carbohydrates: 16.88

Beef Breakfast Casserole

Preparation Time: 10 minutes
Cooking Time: 30 minutes
Servings: 5
Ingredients:
1. 1 pound of ground beef, cooked
2. 10 eggs
3. ½ cup Pico de Gallo
4. 1 cup baby spinach
5. ¼ cup sliced black olives
6. Freshly ground black pepper

Directions:
- Preheat oven to 350 degrees Fahrenheit. Prepare a 9" glass pie plate with non-stick spray.
- Whisk the eggs until frothy. Season with salt and pepper.
- Layer the cooked ground beef, Pico de Gallo, and spinach in the pie plate.
- Slowly pour the eggs over the top.
- Top with black olives.
- Bake for at least 30 minutes, until firm in the middle.
- Slice into 5 pieces and serve.

Nutrition:
Calories: 479 kcal
Protein: 43.54 g
Fat: 30.59 g
Carbohydrates: 4.65 g

Ham and Veggie Frittata Muffins

Preparation Time: 10 minutes
Cooking Time: 25 minutes
Servings: 12
Ingredients:
1. 5 ounces thinly sliced ham
2. 8 large eggs
3. 4 tablespoons coconut oil
4. ½ yellow onion, finely diced
5. 8 oz. frozen spinach, thawed and drained
6. 8 oz. mushrooms, thinly sliced
7. 1 cup cherry tomatoes, halved
8. ¼ cup coconut milk (canned)
9. 2 tablespoons coconut flour
10. Sea salt and pepper to taste

Directions:
- Preheat oven to 375 degrees Fahrenheit.
- In a medium skillet, warm the coconut oil on medium heat. Add the onion and cook until softened.
- Add the mushrooms, spinach, and cherry tomatoes. Season with salt and pepper. Cook until the mushrooms have softened. About 5 minutes. Remove from heat and set aside.
- In a huge bowl, beat the eggs together with the coconut milk and coconut flour. Stir in the cooled the veggie mixture.
- Line each cavity of a 12 cavity muffin tin with the thinly sliced ham. Pour the egg mixture into each one and bake for 20 minutes.
- Remove from oven and allow to cool for about 5 minutes before transferring to a wire rack.
- To maximize the benefit of a vegetable-rich diet, it's important to eat a variety of colors, and these veggie-packed frittata muffins do just that. The onion, spinach, mushrooms, and cherry tomatoes provide a wide range of vitamins and nutrients and a healthy dose of fiber.

Nutrition:
Calories: 125 kcal
Protein: 5.96 g
Fat: 9.84 g

Carbohydrates: 4.48 g

Tomato and Avocado Omelet

Preparation Time: 5 minutes
Cooking Time: 5 minutes
Servings: 1
Ingredients:
1. 2 eggs
2. ¼ avocado, diced
3. 4 cherry tomatoes, halved
4. 1 tablespoon cilantro, chopped
5. Squeeze of lime juice
6. Pinch of salt

Directions:
- Put together the avocado, tomatoes, cilantro, lime juice, and salt in a small bowl, then mix well and set aside.
- Warm a medium nonstick skillet on medium heat. Whisk the eggs until frothy and add to the pan. Move the eggs around gently with a rubber spatula until they begin to set.
- Scatter the avocado mixture over half of the omelet. Remove from heat, and slide the omelet onto a plate as you fold it in half.
- Serve immediately.

Nutrition:
Calories: 433 kcal
Protein: 25.55 g
Fat: 32.75 g
Carbohydrates: 10.06 g

Vegan-Friendly Banana Bread

Preparation Time: 15 minutes
Cooking Time: 40 minutes
Servings: 4-6
Ingredients:
1. 2 ripe bananas, mashed
2. 1/3 cup brewed coffee
3. 3 tbsp. chia seeds
4. 6 tbsp. water
5. ½ cup soft vegan butter
6. ½ cup maple syrup
7. 2 cups flour
8. 2 tsp. baking powder
9. 1 tsp. cinnamon powder
10. 1 tsp. allspice
11. ½ tsp. salt

Directions:
- Set oven at 350F.
- Bring the chia seeds in a small bowl then soak it with 6 tbsp. of water. Stir well and set aside.
- In a mixing bowl, mix using a hand mixer the vegan butter and maple syrup until it turns fluffy. Add the chia seeds along with the mashed bananas.
- Mix well and then add the coffee.
- Meanwhile, sift all the dry ingredients (flour, baking powder, cinnamon powder, all spice, and salt) and then gradually add into the bowl with the wet ingredients.
- Combine the ingredients well and then pour over a baking pan lined with parchment paper.
- Place in the oven to bake for at least 30-40 minutes, or until the toothpick comes out clean after inserting in the bread.
- Allow the bread to cool before serving.

Nutrition:
Calories: 371 kcal
Protein: 5.59 g
Fat: 16.81 g
Carbohydrates: 49.98 g

Mango Granola

Preparation Time: 10 minutes
Cooking Time: 30 minutes
Servings: 4
Ingredients:
1. 2 cups rolled oats
2. 1 cup dried mango, chopped
3. ½ cup almonds, roughly chopped
4. ½ cup nuts
5. ½ cup dates, roughly chopped
6. 3 tbsp. sesame seeds
7. 2 tsp. cinnamon
8. 2/3 cup agave nectar
9. 2 tbsp. coconut oil
10. 2 tbsp. water

Directions:
- Set oven at 320F
- In a large bowl, put the oats, almonds, nuts, sesame seeds, dates, and cinnamon then mix well.
- Meanwhile, heat a saucepan over medium heat, pour in the agave syrup, coconut oil, and water.
- Stir and let it cook for at least 3 minutes or until the coconut oil has melted.
- Gradually pour the syrup mixture into the bowl with the oats and nuts and stir well, ensure that all the ingredients are coated with the syrup.
- Transfer the granola on a baking sheet lined with parchment paper and place in the oven to bake for 20 minutes.
- After 20 minutes, take off the tray from the oven and lay the chopped dried mango on top. Put back in the oven then bake again for another 5 minutes.
- Let the granola cool to room temperature before serving or placing it in an airtight container for storage. The shelf life of the granola will last up to 2-3 weeks.

Nutrition:
Calories: 434 kcal
Protein: 13.16 g

Fat: 28.3 g
Carbohydrates: 55.19 g

Sautéed Veggies on Hot Bagels

Preparation Time: 10 minutes
Cooking Time: 16 minutes
Servings: 2
Ingredients:
1. 1 yellow squash, diced
2. 1 zucchini, sliced thin
3. ½ onion, sliced thin
4. 2 pcs. tomatoes, sliced
5. 1 clove of garlic, chopped
6. salt and pepper to taste
7. 1 tbsp. olive oil
8. 2 pcs. vegan bagels
9. vegan butter for spread

Directions:
- Heat the olive oil on the medium temperature in a cast-iron skillet.
- Lower the heat to medium-low and sauté the onions for 10 minutes or until the onions start to brown.
- Turn the heat again to medium and then add the diced squash and zucchini to the pan and cook for 5 minutes. Add the clove of garlic and cook for another minute.
- Throw in the tomato slices to the pan and cook for 1 minute. Season with pepper and salt and turn off the heat.
- Toast the bagels and cut in half.
- Spread the bagels lightly with butter and serve with the sautéed veggies on top.

Nutrition:
Calories: 375 kcal
Protein: 14.69 g
Fat: 11.46 g
Carbohydrates: 54.61 g

Coco-Tapioca Bowl

Preparation Time: 10 minutes
Cooking Time: 20 minutes
Servings: 2
Ingredients:
1. ¼ cup tapioca pearls, small sized
2. 1 can light coconut milk
3. ¼ cup maple syrup
4. 1 ½ tsp. lemon juice
5. ½ cup unsweetened coconut flakes, toasted
6. 2 cups water

Directions:
- Place the tapioca in a saucepan and pour over the 2 cups of water. Let it stand for at least 30 minutes.
- Pour in the coconut milk and syrup and heat the saucepan over medium temperature. Bring to a boil while stirring constantly.
- Add the lemon juice and stir and then garnish with coconut flakes.

Nutrition:
Calories: 309 kcal
Protein: 3.93 g
Fat: 9.02 g
Carbohydrates: 54.55 g

Choco-Banana Oats

Preparation Time: 5 minutes
Cooking Time: 8 minutes
Servings: 2
Ingredients:
1. 2 cups oats
2. 2 cups almond milk
3. ¾ cup water
4. 2 ripe bananas, sliced
5. ¼ tsp. Vanilla
6. ¼ tsp. almond extract
7. 2 tbsp. cocoa powder, unsweetened
8. 2 tbsp. agave nectar
9. 1/8 tsp. cinnamon
10. 1/8 tsp. salt
11. 1/3 cup toasted walnuts, chopped
12. 2 tbsp. vegan chocolate chips, semisweet

Directions:
- In a large saucepan, pour the almond milk, water, bananas, vanilla, and almond extract. Add the salt, stir, and heat over high temperature.
- Mix the oats in the pan along with the unsweetened cocoa powder, 1 tbsp. agave nectar and lower the temperature to medium. Cook for 7-8 minutes, or until the oats are cooked to your liking. Stir frequently.
- Scoop the cooked oats into serving bowls and garnish with the chopped walnuts, chocolate chips, and drizzle with the remaining agave nectar.

Nutrition:
Calories: 522 kcal
Protein: 30.17 g
Fat: 27.01 g
Carbohydrates: 79.09 g

Savory Bread

Preparation Time: 10 minutes

Cooking Time: 20-25 minutes
Servings: 8-10
Ingredients:

1. ½ cup plus 1tablespoon almond flour
2. 1 tsp. baking soda
3. 1 teaspoon ground turmeric
4. Salt, to taste
5. 2 large organic eggs
6. 2 organic egg whites
7. 1 cup raw cashew butter
8. 1 tablespoon water
9. 1 tablespoon apple cider vinegar

Directions:

- Set the oven to 350F. Grease a loaf pan.
- In a big pan, mix together flour, baking soda, turmeric, and salt.
- In another bowl, add eggs, egg whites, and cashew butter and beat till smooth.
- Gradually, add water and beat till well combined.
- Add flour mixture and mix till well combined.
- Stir in apple cider vinegar treatment.
- Place a combination into prepared loaf pan evenly.
- Bake for around twenty minutes or till a toothpick inserted within the center is released clean.

Nutrition:
Calories: 347
Fat: 11g
Carbohydrates: 29g
Fiber: 6g
Protein: 21g

Savory Veggie Muffins

Preparation Time: 15 minutes
Cooking Time: 18-23 minutes
Servings: 5
Ingredients:
1. ¾ cup almond meal
2. ½ tsp baking soda
3. ¼ cup concentrate powder
4. 2 teaspoons fresh dill, chopped
5. Salt, to taste
6. 4 large organic eggs
7. 1½ tablespoons nutritional yeast
8. 2 teaspoons apple cider vinegar
9. 3 tablespoons fresh lemon juice
10. 2 tablespoons coconut oil, melted
11. 1 cup coconut butter, softened
12. 1 bunch scallion, chopped
13. 2 medium carrots, peeled and grated
14. ½ cup fresh parsley, chopped

Directions:
- Set the oven to 350F. Grease 10 cups of your large muffin tin.
- In a large bowl, mix together flour, baking soda, Protein powder, and salt.
- In another bowl, add eggs, nutritional yeast, vinegar, lemon juice, and oil and beat till well combined.
- Add coconut butter and beat till the mixture becomes smooth.
- Put egg mixture into the flour mixture and mix till well combined.
- Fold in scallion, carts, and parsley.
- Place the amalgamation into prepared muffin cups evenly.
- Bake for about 18-23 minutes or till a toothpick inserted inside center comes out clean.

Nutrition:
Calories: 378
Fat: 13g
Carbohydrates: 32g
Fiber: 11g

Protein: 32g

Crepes with Coconut Cream & Strawberry Sauce

Preparation Time: 15 minutes
Cooking Time: 8 minutes
Servings: 4
Ingredients:
1. For Sauce:
2. 12-ounces frozen strawberries, thawed and liquid reserved
3. 1½ teaspoons tapioca starch
4. 1 tablespoon honey
5. For the Coconut cream:
6. 1 (13½-ounce) can chilled coconut milk
7. 1 teaspoon organic vanilla flavoring
8. 1 tablespoon organic honey
9. For Crepes:
10. 2 tablespoons tapioca starch
11. 2 tablespoons coconut flour
12. ¼ cup almond milk
13. 2 organic eggs
14. Pinch of salt
15. Avocado oil, as required

Directions:
- For sauce inside a bowl, mix together some reserved strawberry liquid and tapioca starch.
- Add remaining ingredients and mix well.
- Transfer a combination inside a pan on medium-high heat.
- Bring to a boil, stirring continuously.
- Cook for at least 2-3 minutes, till the sauce, becomes thick.
- Remove from heat and aside, covered till serving.
- For coconut cream, carefully, scoop your cream from your surface of a can of coconut milk.
- In a mixer, add coconut cream, vanilla flavoring, and honey and pulse for around 6-8 minutes or till fluffy.
- For crepes in a blender, add all ingredients and pulse till well combined and smooth.
- Lightly, grease a substantial nonstick skillet with avocado oil as well as heat on medium-low heat.

- Add a modest amount of mixture and tilt the pan to spread it evenly inside the skillet.
- Cook approximately 1-2 minutes.
- Carefully change the side and cook for approximately 1-1½ minutes more.
- Repeat with the remaining mixture.
- Divide the coconut cream onto each crepe evenly and fold into quarters.
- Place strawberry sauce ahead and serve.

Nutrition:
Calories: 364
 Fat: 9g
Carbohydrates: 26g
Fiber: 7g
 Protein: 15g

Spicy Ginger Crepes

Preparation Time: 15 minutes
Cooking Time: 20-30 seconds
Servings: 8
Ingredients:
1. 1 1/3 cups chickpea flour
2. ½ teaspoon red chili powder
3. Salt, to taste
4. 1 (1-inch) fresh ginger piece, grated finely
5. 1 cup fresh cilantro leaves, chopped
6. 1 green chili, seeded and chopped finely
7. 1 cup water
8. Cooking spray, as required

Directions:
- In a sizable bowl, mix together flour, chili powder, and salt.
- Add ginger, cilantro, and chili and mix well.
- Add water and mix till an even mixture form.
- Keep aside, covered for approximately ½-120 minutes.
- Lightly, grease a substantial nonstick skillet with cooking spray and heat on medium-high heat.
- Add the desired volume of the mixture and tilt the pan to spread it evenly inside the skillet.
- Cook approximately 10-15 seconds per side.
- Repeat while using the remaining mixture.

Nutrition:
Calories: 73
Fat: 1.3
 Carbohydrates: 11g
 Fiber: 2.1g,
Protein: 4.3g

Honey Pancakes

Preparation Time: 10 minutes
Cooking Time: 5 minutes
Servings: 2
Ingredients:
1. ½ cup almond flour
2. 2 tablespoons coconut flour
3. 1 tablespoon ground flaxseeds
4. ¼ tsp baking soda
5. ½ tablespoon ground ginger
6. ½ tablespoon ground nutmeg
7. ½ tablespoon ground cinnamon
8. ½ teaspoon ground cloves
9. Pinch of salt
10. 2 tablespoons organic honey
11. ¾ cup organic egg whites
12. ½ teaspoon organic vanilla extract
13. Coconut oil, as required

Directions:
- In a big bowl, mix together flours, flax seeds, baking soda, spices, and salt.
- In another bowl, add honey, egg whites and vanilla and beat till well combined.
- Put the egg mixture into the flour mixture then mix till well combined.
- Lightly, grease a big nonstick skillet with oil and heat on medium-low heat.
- Add about ¼ cup of mixture and tilt the pan to spread it evenly inside the skillet.
- Cook for about 3-4 minutes.
- Carefully, customize the side and cook approximately 1 minute more.
- Repeat with the remaining mixture.
- Serve along with your desired topping.

Nutrition:
Calories: 291
Fat: 8g

Carbohydrates: 26g
 Fiber: 4g
Protein: 23g

Cilantro Pancakes

Preparation Time: 10 minutes
Cooking Time: 6-8 minutes
Servings: 6
Ingredients:
1. ½ cup tapioca flour
2. ½ cup almond flour
3. ½ teaspoon chili powder
4. ¼ teaspoon ground turmeric
5. Salt, to taste
6. Freshly ground black pepper, to taste
7. 1 cup full- fat coconut milk
8. ½ of red onion, chopped
9. 1 (½-inch) fresh ginger piece, grated finely
10. 1 Serrano pepper, minced
11. ½ cup fresh cilantro, chopped
12. Oil, as required

Directions:
- In a big bowl, put together the flours and spices then mix.
- Put the coconut milk and mix till well combined.
- Fold within the onion, ginger, Serrano pepper, and cilantro.
- Lightly, grease a sizable nonstick skillet with oil and warmth on medium-low heat.
- Add about ¼ cup of mixture and tilt the pan to spread it evenly inside the skillet.
- Cook for around 3-4 minutes from either side.
- Repeat with all the remaining mixture.
- Serve along with your desired topping.

Nutrition:
Calories: 331
Fat: 10g
Carbohydrates: 37g
Fiber: 6g
Protein: 28g

Zucchini Pancakes

Preparation Time: 15 minutes
Cooking Time: 6-10 min
Servings: 8
Ingredients:
1. 1 cup chickpea flour
2. 1½ cups water, divided
3. ¼ teaspoon cumin seeds
4. ¼ tsp cayenne
5. ¼ teaspoon ground turmeric
6. Salt, to taste
7. ½ cup zucchini, shredded
8. ½ cup red onion, chopped finely
9. 1 green chile, seeded and chopped finely
10. ¼ cup fresh cilantro, chopped

Directions:
- In a large bowl, add flour and ¾ cup with the water and beat till smooth.
- Add remaining water and beat till a thin
- Fold inside the onion, ginger, Serrano pepper, and cilantro.
- Lightly, grease a substantial nonstick skillet with oil and heat on medium-low heat.
- Add about ¼ cup of mixture and tilt the pan to spread it evenly in the skillet.
- Cook for around 4-6 minutes.
- Carefully, alter the side and cook for approximately 2-4 minutes.
- Repeat while using the remaining mixture.
- Serve together with your desired topping.

Nutrition:
Calories: 389
Fat: 13g
Carbohydrates: 25g
Fiber: 4g
Protein: 21g

Pumpkin & Banana Waffles

Preparation Time: 15 minutes
Cooking Time: 5 minutes
Servings: 4
Ingredients:
1. ½ cup almond flour
2. ½ cup coconut flour
3. 1 tsp baking soda
4. 1½ teaspoons ground cinnamon
5. ¾ teaspoon ground ginger
6. ½ teaspoon ground cloves
7. ½ teaspoon ground nutmeg
8. Salt, to taste
9. 2 tablespoons olive oil
10. 5 large organic eggs
11. ¾ cup almond milk
12. ½ cup pumpkin puree
13. 2 medium bananas, peeled and sliced

Directions:
- Preheat the waffle iron, and after that, grease it.
- In a sizable bowl, mix together flours, baking soda, and spices.
- In a blender, put the remaining ingredients and pulse till smooth.
- Add flour mixture and pulse till
- In preheated waffle iron, add the required quantity of mixture.
- Cook approximately 4-5 minutes.
- Repeat using the remaining mixture.

Nutrition:
Calories: 357.2
Fat: 28.5g
Carbohydrates: 19.7g
Fiber: 4g
Protein: 14g

Blueberry & Cashew Waffles

Preparation Time: 15 minutes
Cooking Time: 4-5 minutes
Servings: 5
Ingredients:

1. 1 cup raw cashews
2. 3 tablespoons coconut flour
3. 1 tsp baking soda
4. Salt, to taste
5. ½ cup unsweetened almond milk
6. 3 organic eggs
7. ¼ cup coconut oil, melted
8. 3 tablespoons organic honey
9. ½ teaspoon organic vanilla flavor
10. 1 cup fresh blueberries

Directions:

- Preheat the waffle iron after which grease it.
- In a mixer, add cashews and pulse till flour-like consistency forms.
- Transfer the cashew flour in a big bowl.
- Add almond flour, baking soda and salt and mix well.
- In another bowl, put the remaining ingredients and beat till well combined.
- Put the egg mixture into the flour mixture then mix till well combined.
- Fold in blueberries.
- In preheated waffle iron, add the required amount of mixture.
- Cook for around 4-5 minutes.
- Repeat with the remaining mixture.

Nutrition:
Calories: 432
Fat: 32
Carbohydrates: 32g
Protein: 13g

Cheddar and Chive Souffles

Preparation Time: 10 minutes
Cooking Time: 25 minutes
Servings: 8
Ingredients:
1. ½ cup almond flour
2. ¼ cup chopped chives
3. 1 tsp salt
4. ½ tsp xanthan gum
5. 1 tsp ground mustard
6. ¼ tsp cayenne pepper
7. ½ tsp cracked black pepper
8. ¾ cup heavy cream
9. 2 cups shredded cheddar cheese
10. ½ cup baking powder
11. 6 organic eggs, separated

Directions:
- Switch on the oven, then set its temperature to 350°F and let it preheat.
- Take a medium bowl, add flour in it, add remaining ingredients, except for baking powder and eggs, and whisk until combined.
- Separate egg yolks and egg whites between two bowls, add egg yolks in the flour mixture and whisk until incorporated.
- Add baking powder into the egg whites and beat with an electric mixer until stiff peaks form and then stir egg whites into the flour mixture until well mixed.
- Divide the batter evenly between eight ramekins and then bake for 25 minutes until done.
- Serve straight away or store in the refrigerator until ready to eat.

Nutrition:
Calories 288
Total Fat 21g
Total Carbs 3g
Protein 14g

Cheesy Flax and Hemp Seeds Muffins

Preparation Time: 5 minutes
Cooking Time: 30 minutes
Servings: 2
Ingredients:

1. 1/8 cup flax seeds meal
2. ¼ cup raw hemp seeds
3. ¼ cup almond meal
4. Salt, to taste
5. ¼ tsp baking powder
6. 3 organic eggs, beaten
7. 1/8 cup nutritional yeast flakes
8. ¼ cup cottage cheese, low-fat
9. ¼ cup grated parmesan cheese
10. ¼ cup scallion, sliced thinly
11. 1 tbsp. olive oil

Directions:

- Switch on the oven, then set it 360°F and let it preheat.
- Meanwhile, take two ramekins, grease them with oil, and set aside until required.
- Take a medium bowl, add flax seeds, hemp seeds, and almond meal, and then stir in salt and baking powder until mixed.
- Crack eggs in another bowl, add yeast, cottage cheese, and parmesan, stir well until combined, and then stir this mixture into the almond meal mixture until incorporated.
- Fold in scallions, then distribute the mixture between prepared ramekins and bake for 30 minutes until muffins are firm and the top is nicely golden brown.
- When done, take out the muffins from the ramekins and let them cool completely on a wire rack.
- For meal prepping, wrap each muffin with a paper towel and refrigerate for up to thirty-four days.
- When ready to eat, reheat muffins in the microwave until hot and then serve.

Nutrition:
Calories 179
Total Fat 10.9g

Total Carbs 6.9g
Protein 15.4g
Sugar 2.3g
Sodium 311mg

Fantastic Spaghetti Squash with Cheese and Basil Pesto

Preparation Time: 10 minutes
Cooking Time: 35 minutes
Servings: 2
Ingredients:
1. 1 cup cooked spaghetti squash, drained
2. Salt, to taste
3. Freshly cracked black pepper, to taste
4. ½ tbsp. olive oil
5. ¼ cup ricotta cheese, unsweetened
6. 2oz fresh mozzarella cheese, cubed
7. 1/8 cup basil pesto

Directions:
- Switch on the oven, then set its temperature to 375 °F and let it preheat.
- Meanwhile, take a medium bowl, add spaghetti squash in it and then season with salt and black pepper.
- Take a casserole dish, grease it with oil, add squash mixture in it, top it with ricotta cheese and mozzarella cheese and bake for 10 minutes until cooked.
- When done, remove the casserole dish from the oven, drizzle pesto on top and serve immediately.

Nutrition:
Calories 169
Total Fat 11.3g
Total Carbs 6.2g
Protein 11.9g
Sugar 0.1g
Sodium 217mg

Flaxseed Porridge with Cinnamon

Preparation Time: 10 minutes
Cooking Time: 5 minutes
Servings: 4
Ingredients:
1. 1 tsp cinnamon
2. 1½ tsp stevia
3. 1 tbsp. unsalted butter
4. 2 tbsp. flaxseed meal
5. 2 tbsp. flaxseed oatmeal
6. ½ cup shredded coconut
7. 1 cup heavy cream
8. 2 cups of water

Directions:
- Take a medium pot, place it over low heat, add all the ingredients in it, stir until mixed and bring the mixture to boil.
- When the mixture has boiled, remove the pot from heat, stir it well and divide it evenly between four bowls.
- Let porridge rest for 10 minutes until slightly thicken and then serve.

Nutrition:
Calories 171
Total Fat 16g
Total Carbs 6g
Protein 2g

Shirataki Pasta with Avocado and Cream

Preparation Time: 10 minutes
Cooking Time: 6 minutes
Servings: 2
Ingredients:

1. ½ packet of shirataki noodles, cooked
2. ½ of an avocado
3. ½ tsp cracked black pepper
4. ½ tsp salt
5. ½ tsp dried basil
6. 1/8 cup heavy cream

Directions:

- Place a medium pot half full with water over medium heat, bring it to boil, then add noodles and cook for 2 minutes.
- Then drain the noodles and set aside until required.
- Place avocado in a bowl, mash it with a fork,
- Mash avocado in a bowl, transfer it in a blender, add remaining ingredients, and pulse until smooth.
- Take a frying pan, place it over medium heat and when hot, add noodles in it, pour in the avocado mixture, stir well and cook for 2 minutes until hot.
- Serve straight away.

Nutrition:
Calories 131
Total Fat 12.6g
Total Carbs 4.9g
Protein 1.2g
Sugar 0.3g
Sodium 588mg

Cinnamon Pancakes with Coconut

Preparation Time: 5 minutes
Cooking Time: 18 minutes
Servings: 2
Ingredients:

1. 2 organic eggs
2. 1 tbsp. almond flour
3. 2oz cream cheese
4. ¼ cup shredded coconut and more for garnishing
5. ½ tbsp. erythritol
6. 1/8 tsp salt
7. 1 tsp cinnamon
8. 4 tbsp. stevia
9. ½ tbsp. olive oil

Directions:

- Crack eggs in a bowl, beat until fluffy and then beat in flour and cream cheese until smooth.
- Add remaining ingredients and then stir until well combined.
- Take a frying pan, place it over medium heat, grease it with oil, then pour in half of the batter and cook for 3 to 4 minutes per side until the pancake has cooked and nicely golden brown.
- Transfer pancake to a plate and cook another pancake in the same manner by using the remaining batter.
- Sprinkle coconut on top of cooked pancakes and serve.

Nutrition:
Calories 575
Total Fat 51g
Total Carbs 3.5g
Protein 19g

Banana Cashew Toast

Preparation Time: 10 minutes
Cooking Time: 0 minutes
Servings: 3
Ingredients:

1. 1 cup roasted cashews (unsalted)

2. 4 pieces oat bread
3. 2 ripe medium-sized bananas
4. Dash of salt
5. Pinch of cinnamon
6. 2 tsp. flax meals
7. 2 tsp. honey

Directions:

- Peel and slice the bananas into ½-inch pieces. Toast the bread. In a food processor, puree the salt and cashews until they are smooth. Use the puree as a spread on the toasts. On top of the spread, arrange a layer of bananas. Add flax meals and a dash of cinnamon on top of the bananas. Top the toast with honey.

Nutrition:

Calories: 634 kcal
Protein: 13.42 g
Fat: 47.6 g
Carbohydrates: 48.02 g

Apple Oatmeal

Preparation Time: 10 minutes
Cooking Time: 5 minutes
Servings: 2
Ingredients:
1. 2/3 cups rolled oats
2. 1 cup water
3. 1 teaspoon ground cinnamon
4. 1 cup of any non-fat milk, coconut milk or almond milk (optional)
5. ¼ cup fresh apple juice
6. 1 chopped apple, (unpeeled or peeled)

Directions:
- Place the water, juice, and the apple in a deep pot. Bring to boil over medium heat.
- Add the oats and cinnamon. Bring to another boil. Lower the heat temperature and let it simmer for 3 minutes or until it is thick.
- Divide the serving into two and serve with milk.

Nutrition:
Calories: 277 kcal
Protein: 12.69 g
Fat: 7.69 g
Carbohydrates: 52.71 g

Strawberry Yogurt treat

Preparation Time: 10 minutes
Cooking Time: 0 minutes
Servings: 2
Ingredients:
1. 4 cups 0% fat plain yogurt
2. 1 cup sliced strawberries
3. 8 tbsp. of flax meal
4. 4 tbsp. honey
5. 8 tbsp. walnuts (chopped)

Directions:
- Distribute 2 cups of the yogurt into your serving bowls. Neatly layer the flax meal and the walnut in the middle. Add a drizzle of half of the honey before covering with the last layer of yogurt. Add the honey on top of the yogurt to add color when you serve.

Nutrition:
Calories: 733 kcal
Protein: 38.42 g
Fat: 30.57 g
Carbohydrates: 83.44 g